KW-585-042

The Beckwalker

and other poems

MICHAEL FFINCH

LATIMER

First published in 1977
by Latimer New Dimensions Limited
14 West Central Street, London WC1A 1JH

© 1977, Michael Ffinch

SBN 901539 60 0

Printed and bound in Great Britain
by Villiers Publications Ltd, Ingestre Road, London NW5

Poetry Library
105898

COPY NO. 2

THE ARTS COUNCIL OF GREAT BRITAIN
POETRY LIBRARY
105 PICCADILLY, LONDON, W1V OAU
DATE DUE BACK

3 JAN 1978		
12 OCT 1978		
17 AUG 1982		
2 APR 1993		

The Beckwalker
and other poems

for my Father
ROBERT MAULE FFINCH
1903 - 1975

Contents

Acknowledgments

Some of these poems have appeared in *Keats Memorial Poems, The Worth Record,* and *Carols for Children.*

Simon's Garden was written for, and first performed by the Boys of Worth School in March 1973. It will be broadcast by the B.B.C. during Holy Week in 1977 with music composed by Francis Shaw.

The Undertaker Poet was first published in a limited edition in 1968 with illustrations by Zena Tibbenham.

The anthem *Maria* was written for the Consecration of Worth Abbey Church and set to music by Dom. Philip Gaisford, O.S.B.

by the same author
Voices round a Star (1970)

The Beckwalker

Consonous, continuous,
fierce and deep after a full rain,
though skater-callous
ever a neighbour, friend to the three farms
that make you turn no mill, no turbine,
but strain for tank and cistern close
above the cow line;
what little that means of all you churn,
chutter-guggle, forcely

down Straddle Fall, our pool
for summer swims; or tear of winter
sticks, turf, barbed-off wool,
fertiliser bags impale on sallows,
Lunewards, seaward. Ceaseless, never
intrusive your jargon, a lull,
a soothing persuader
in permanence that cheerfully slows
each turmoil to coolness,

clearness. Whether upfell
where your oozey rises give race
into Bowderdale,
or down through meadowsweet runs, willow lands
where Athol trains his dogs, you speak
of concord, Minder of Marvels,
that we the Shallow-Sick
Ones so narrowly understand;
constant the telling,

casual the response,
though we would take from your swift turns,
rolls, whirls, recompense.
Here where you left wearings in the limestone,
there you let erratic granite
fling you westward in a trounce,
twist, part, then unite
that rains might flood to oxbow;
which much convinces

that our will not free
would be sheer unrolling, as your spate
our insecurity.
But Choosers we are made, whose Love-Arbiter
still persists; all this intricate
idea, here found fact in every
eddy-angle, straight,
or curve-meander, gives fuller
merit to our being

who can see set symbol
in your clear exceeding, made on
might invisible,
who find your forms confirm our deepest dare,
with no return, as once a Whitsun
beck-walk was for friends a special
wakening, was seen
immense the wholeness in the share
that makes us holy,

certain. Deep in your run
we meet the same estranging darkness:
stones mottled, sunken
like a toad's back; winter weed, flow-combed, burned
black at the snow. So too your secrets bless

into radiance: what lies hidden
is not fearful; loss
what was never needed or earned;
our cravings heinous

mostly. In its mystery
join us on the journey, blest
waters seem to say.
Whether lace frosts embitter
into tractor bearing ice, or August
droughts dimute us to a trickle
we take our end on trust
that some rich trace of what we were
will reach the sea.

Wild Boar Fell

A curlew by the roadside makes me pause
And curiously I wait to watch it fly;
Four white fell-ponies nod up, swing away,
In crooked file they trek on up the moor,

Till horseless, birdless, I am left to see
How wall-decked Mallerstang lies deep in haze
With field and farmhouse backed by ash and elms
Burnt-brown as rushes in this April heat

Below; there once the Eden rose to moat
Round wrecked Pendragon, soon to be restored,
Though little less must be this valley since

de Morville restless one full Easter night
Sought out the rising blackness of Wild Boar
Found Becket's profile there and fled for France.

David's Line

This Christmas I am early out to cut
   the thyme, and parsley by the drystone wall
   is frosty, crisp to hand. Beyond, the full
cow-steamy byre and ponies puzzled out

in brume. A mistmoon beams, asserts the ash
   above the corner of our oval garth,
   seals mystery round the cobbled yard beneath.
I clutch the herbs and make a Christmas wish.

How all is still. The silence is immense,
   till from the toppled shed a cockerel crows
informing farms how one escaped the kill,

that, with a shudder, I am out of trance
   aware of motion merging on my gaze,
see sheep, a shepherd striding from the fell.

The Gill

for Simon

Deluge, cloudburst or downpour, scud or shower
  sends each cart-track scurrying
—fall and rivulet each small dint and gully—
  down to the place where two becks meet.

This gill, sodden now, where you and I walked,
  son and father, looking for leaves,
fishes, anything we might take home smiling,
  our experience only;

both collectors of random rocks and flowers
  by this your stream, sunshine then.
I, today alone, find each step extended :
  to you, of course; but similar

moments too through my childhood's secret conduit :
  me fishing, my first water-chute;
more, still frightening : spitfires, shrapnel, flashes,
  blasts that shook the plover's eggs,

sirens shinning me down from rick or tree-house.
  Once with London blazing, I
in my dressing-gown watched the sunset city,
  eyes adaze with Their's and Our's. Was

fear in everything hoaxing smiles and glances?
  With a firm horror to fix to :
from the Anderson, whispers, silence, Dornier's
  drunning, fear was understood.

So we comfortably set the cause at something
far, very far from ouselves,
shunning always the balanced voice insisting
we shoulder universal blame:

war as error in me, in brother, father,
grandfather, all those great-great-greats.
Not in They; but in They as well as always
Us, Simon, and in summer.

Is this possibly why now, hearing water
guggling, boom down rock-slides, I
stiffen, anxiously scan the banks for shelter,
search the granite clouds for squadrons?

Barbed instinctively by our panic's basis
we see similar attitudes:
sullen, rational motives dull with history
striding clenched-fist at failure;

clump-clod-hoppering hatreds, envies stud their
ample-regular patterns.
How persuasively each sure sign is muffled:
"It could never happen again,

never happen again!" As prophets, augurs
count the days, high on the fell-steps
one poet carefully wracking forcible words
with which to quell his anguish

will most certainly stumble past unnoticed;
who feels there will be water
in the infinite calm oasis; finding
more marvels in the fine fact

that a peckishsome heron gauntly stalking
   Bowderdale Beck for tiddlers
will fly carrying salmon spawn to stretches
   no fish could ever conquer,

leaves determinist logic slammed in cell-block
   prose, desolate, starved. (Nature,
unpredictable, we may merely follow,
   watch adoringly, our fellow

traveller in this constant full adventure,
   like us fallen and dependent,
as perfected, we beg, on Finding-Out Day.)
   Such, dear Simon, is your Father.

The Dipper

for Jonathan

Recalling how one Nature Trail through Dovedale
   was wrecked because I did not see the Dipper,
   ("Ffinch is sick he did not see that Dipper, Sir!"
two sneaks, anoraked, had told the Holy Moule)

I feel today some scar-fading merriment:
   I have one to myself. Low-skimming the beck
   it passes me, pert white bib at the neck,
to settle on a race-swirled stone adjacent

the ferny crevice it, last year, brooded in.
   Bobbing now for beetles or boatmen it stays,
scans a moment, then dives. I walk on downstream

the brighter, seeing light in Lunesdale redden
   to autumn dusk, thankful that memories can rise,
for calm, a diving bird, for my make in time.

The Dowly Tree

At dusk, the last night of the year, I climb
   to reach the Dowly Tree. As startled sheep
   skip further up the scree, I make my claim
gripping the lichened bark. How ice-winds nip

between my body and the squall-bent bole.
   Seeming oddly secure upon this Scar,
   weird, wild tree, seeded by some owl
that ripping crop or gizzard dropped you here;

or else the searing wind that chops the tarn.
   Maybe the broad-winged buzzard took some part.
Whatever origin, you stand alone

protesting life, stability, in turn.
   A poet is like you in his questing heart
redeeming words from harsh, eroded stone.

Bowderdale

Memo to R.M.Ff.

1

The Abbey clock strikes eight; only now am I
free to tap out a message : two tired children
abed, supper done, the cooker stoked and riddled.
   Those cars on our road,

distracting for a moment, handy, I make
one hurtle my thought-line up the motorway.
Stony Stratford, Skelmersdale and Lancaster
   smartly past aside,

till turned off where the Lune Valley meets Tebay
I take that last stretch through the railway cuttings
down to Mason's farm; soon in front of me
   find the white-railed bridge

spanning Bowderdale Beck, my symbol of home.
Familiar all now : twin gardened Christmas Trees,
goat's stone and chain, ram's horn on the stable door,
   and corner wall-light

scanning a spoilt Mermaid that boltered to briar.
What other front door could have quite that clanking
welcome as the latch lifts? Quickly I close out
   the October cold

and join you sitting by the fire. Already
a mass of moments jostle for a mention,
but, disciplinarian by profession,
   I am selective;

so taking you with me now on this ramble
through the old times, we are cycling along
the lane to Lalham on a Monday morning,
  and on my shoulder

your firm hand pushing me those last few pedals
on my way to school. Why should you know the pain
at parting that I felt as each week began?
  I never told you,

though I used to wonder if you felt the same;
even today, after some thirty-odd years,
that same home-ache returns at the remembrance
  of those Feltham War years:

our iron garden shelter, the mounted gun
that used to trundle up and down the Hounslow
line, splitting the dull droning of the Dorniers
  trapped in the searchlights.

One night you showed me, from the landing window,
London blazing, rose as an Autumn evening,
while below, flaring incendiaries on the lawn.
  Such sights eternal

now, for we surely find all our memories,
each moment detail-filled, sacred in the end.
Forbid it otherwise; how else should we know
  who we really are?

2

Friendly the darkness; we shut the orchard gate
and take the cart-track falling to the marshes,
a file of Lombardies looms up as we near
   a wide reeded creek

which runs out tidal by the winded sea-wall:
Oxley Marsh behind us, coastguard cottages
far away to the right; forward, Orfordness
   scouring the shingle.

Early September, we watch for the first flights
as smooth mud silvers in a breaking dawn,
tense for whistling teal, or shorebound mallard
   off Turner's stubble.

Then with the light, see close, paralleled dyke-lanes,
the old jetty half sunk in surf-hurled stones,
war wreckage, lookout posts, and beyond, Orford
   Castle, keep and church.

You have often said how hard to turn away
from those free Suffolk days. Boyton and Butley,
dear names now tug at the heart; those stout Punches
   that strained at the plough,

or lumbered wheat-laden wains down David's Lane,
are balance to my mind, bold pointers forward,
matched in permanence with the little graveyard
   where my brother lies.

Inter-City

The Boatbound train made speed; through Bedfordshire
  we shook and swayed. Friesians in buttercups,
  gold banks of gorse, foundries and rubbish tips
flicked by, allotments with the bean-poles bare.

"Last night the Glasgow Sleeper got derailed" :
  Nuneaton now, like Moorgate, Aberfan,
  a name to sear, to meet a sorrow in.
Each time we lurched I found the strangers smiled.

Though set in English silence, each one knew
  what rails the other's silence shuddered on,
and could not settle to a sleep or read.

"How gusts hurl silver on the early corn,"
  I wished to say. A Southbound shivered through.
We smiled, and hurtled on for Holyhead.

The Consumers

After the cleared site
the factories, then the gravel-pit filled in;
the obvious flight
path of the landing jets seemed natural
once I found the hedges gone, the droning din
of dozers, lorries, "Guard Dogs" warning wall:
for this development all plans on show.
Girders, heaps of loam
might contradict, but I am in the know,
here was once our home.

Others there must be
who knew this as the narrow lane, tussocks
of fresh-stooked barley
by the Bedfont road, where we in war-time
watched horse-drawn harvests, brass-nodding forelocks
heaving tall wagons into Feltham farm.
There winter threshing thrilled, the steam machine
wheel-belts shaking slats,
shy palm-fulls, then the chewiness of grain,
mouse nests, chasing rats.

Our thatched chicken hut
chopped from a kennel, all the hens with names,
ration-book diet,
Amercian packages from an aunt,
while on the front lawn incendiary flames
fanned panic as the siren's wailing chaunt,
seem now, serious or trivial, calm naves
to heal the mind in;
certainties that childhood hoarded survive
like suffering gone;

which much providing
why, at my younger brother's grave beneath
wide cedar shading,
where Irish yews grow grand in sentinel,
there on a nearby form a recent wreath,
I see my family knelt in April
grief, just as when over thirty years back
we took the short lane,
walked this same curving country graveyard track
accepting our pain.

Time would persuade me,
though vainly, I trust, to accept set sequence,
but in memory
most order fades; reason mounts subject
to contours where mystery leads, and conscience
rules. Where all is present each thought and act
consort to give account, and this present
will sustain the past.
As the old and dying speak out time spent,
special gifts that last,

that wild-rose garden
where we scavenged windfalls, played he, explored,
now cleared, white wooden
pegs proposing future on its levelled
waste, may grow again rosey, the orchard
plum-heavy, the scent of sage, while I who filled
my mind with wonders can still exclaim
its former glory.
I, at my end perhaps, will need its name,
foist fumitory,

thyme, on those who mind
my ranging last exchanges. Let it be
that in this scarred ground
lie enmangled roots, rotten trellis bars,
brick verges, dozed-out stumps of apple-tree.
Above a factory rises functional, cars
will park in marked-off rows on desolate
concrete surfaces,
and signboards say: Directors Only; neat
the flower-tub terraces.

Though by the lych-gate
from a box bush, how the blackbird sings.
I stare content, wait
until the next plane looms, and feel wild
comfort, hopeful future near. Stillness brings
assurance in. I see how once a child
exploring, wandered into death, whose secret
no-one now may share.
Rest on, unmarked. I never will forget
your dear grave is here.

The Pilgrim

After the march, the last mile with sore feet,
  I reach the Shrine. The Virgin of the Glass
  Wakes in the North her mantle as I pass :
The consummation of four days retreat

To kneel before this Face in candle heat,
  Follow in crudest carving voices, as
  Each feature merges, centres in the Mass.
The eye's achievement on each brow I meet

Transcends all market, custom, politics,
  Where pleading honours, melody commends
Our body's ally when the body dies;

To her I pray, so every heart seems fixed,
  Freed in the flesh to meditate my end,
Appoint all future to her mysteries.

SIMON'S GARDEN

The Garden

Dark is the dark that the fisherman sees,
phosphorescence
waking the waters,
fishscales glisten
silver like leaves.
How was it, Simon, you slept in the garden?
Say, was it comfort,
fatigue?
Was it fear,
faint-hearted intention,
a weak head for wine,
the thought that you still
had your master so near,
could seal you in slumber,
in sleep without care?
He did care,
Simon, we share;
your shame and your sadness
were ours from the start,
in the telling or sorrow we all take a part.
When Man stretched too high
in the joy of his Eden,
wept for his weakness,
lost his possession,
his love became lonely,
his vision obscured;
doubt,
anxiety,
hatred were stirred.
the way of the Worldly became his obsession,
Man made for love
sought his ends in agression.

Through the rough hilly regions
an army advancing,
rumours abound in the squares of the city;
shipments of missiles are piled on the quays,
fighters zoom out
over mine-zoned seas.

I hear children crying,
mothers screaming;
fires flare in the homes of the city;
shots ratter-tatter through the rhythm of feet;
men crumple up
and die in the street.

All this terror
from the world we know.
Is there any peaceful harbour
where the heart may go?
With this famine in the cheeks
and hatred in the eye;
through the clamour and the clanging,
the banners and the banging,
dare Man speak of peace?
Does Peace have to die?

There is one peace only for the heart of Man :
a Love that will love
through the malice of men,
gain back the graces
with which we began.
Love that now watches alone
in the garden.

O who would hold to the night,
the dark,
the desertion?
would pass through the darkness,
would fathom the night?
for the journey of sorrow
is the way to the garden,
the way from the garden, the only light.

It is hard to see in the daunt of the garden,
ghostly,
gargoyles the eyes,
the grimaces;
flames from the torches
draw fear from the faces.
Soldiers well-trained for a scuffle,
a scatter,
stand by a traitor
with cudgels and cord,
strain to support him,
to bludgeon,
to batter,
See him step forward as if he adored.
Simon, Simon, put up your sword!

Judas. Judas.
Judas. Judas.
Judas. Judas.
JUDAS.
Judas was free.
Judas knew,
Judas had worked out what he would do.
There was no movement
Judas would miss,
he had even planned carefully
his callous kiss.
But where was Judas? Judas the child,
the boy who once laughed,
the young man who smiled?
The Judas of vision,
the Judas who wept,
the watcher who waited with John in the wild;
the keeper who prayed,
whose promise was kept?
How could a heart harden that once could accept?
Judas could not accept!
Judas despairing,
damaged and closed,
active and furtive
while loyal friends dozed.
Judas important,
as part of a plan:
chosen to further the future of Man,
Judas was chosen.
Judas chose.

Hard were his thoughts
as he marched with the guards
out from the garrison,
over the ford:
the thirty bright pieces
pouched in his purse,
his soul set on darkness
slid on like a hearse;
a guide through the olive trees
straight to his Lord.
Judas the Traitor will have his reward.

The Pillar

Come out, Simon;
out of the shadows!
Cold is the courtyard,
Sentries are stamping;
Close round neighbourly
near to the firelight;
hear the wood crackling,
watch the flames spiralling.
Simon, the fisherman,
father us, comfort us.
Come out, Simon,
sing us a song;
you who were there
in the walks of the garden:
why are you silent?
Why do you stare?
You were there!
Were there!

Sing us of Abraham,
father of blessings.
Sing us of Abraham,
Searcher of stars.
Sing us of Abraham
exiled in Egypt
Sing us of Abraham,
server of Angels.
Sing us of Abraham
Ishmail and Isaac.
Sing us of Abraham,
pleader for cities.
Sing us of Abraham,
builder of altars.

Sing us of Abraham,
Father of Peoples.

O we carry, Father,
the fire and the faggots:
Where is the lamb
we need for the altar?

God will provide himself
with a lamb,
a lamb for the slaughter.

Tell us of Moses,
who saw he bush blazing.
Tell us of Moses,
who led us from Egypt.
Tell us of Moses,
who parted the waters.
Tell us of Moses,
who prayed on the mountain.
Tell us of Moses,
who gave us commandments.
Tell us of Moses,
who struck the rockface.
Tell us of Moses,
who followed the pillar.
Tell us of Moses,
who raised up the Serpent.
Tell us of Moses,
who showed us our home.

Let us look up,
gaze on the Serpent.
Let us look up,
and be healed.

Sing us of David,
Shepherd and dancer,
Sing us of David,
poet and soldier.
Sing us of David,
Philistine slayer.
Sing us of David,
Father and lover.
Sing us of David
and Jonathan's friendship.
Sing us of David
deposed and in exile.
Sing us of David
taking the shewbread.
Sing us of David
designing the temple.
Sing us of David
Father of Solomon.
Sing us of David
Father of Absolom.
Sing us of David
when Absolom plotted.

O Absolom, my son, my son.
O Absolom, my son.

Tell of Elias,
Prophet of Carmel.
Tell of Elias,
Achab and Jezebel.
Tell of Elias
alone in the desert.
Tell of Elias
under the juniper.

Tell of Elias
fed by the ravens.
Tell of Elias,
the oil and the flour.
Tell of Elias
when fire fell from Heaven.
Tell of Elias
who sought out Elisha.
Tell of Elias
who mantled Elisha.

Lord, I can take no more.
put an end to my life,
my life.

The Crown

The King is coming.
Every head is straining right.
Many of the people here
have waited up all night.
Maps of the Route
hang flapping from their folders;
see the children slither up
on to father's shoulders.
Wave the flags in frenzy;
hold the cameras high,
shout and cheer the carriage
till your throats go dry.
A crowning for the King, my child.
pageantry
and plumes;
with portly Gentlemen-at-Arms
beside the mounted grooms;
with twenty Regimental Bands
well-spaced out on Parade.
O the hours and hours of stitching!
The miles of golden braid!
It was well worth the wait, my child,
the sacrifice we made.

The King is coming!
The Abbey aisles are full.
The ropes up to the belfrey
receive a final pull.
Bishops in embroidered copes
process up to the East;
the Choir ringed round the Sanctuary
prepare "Zadock the Priest".
See the King advancing
as trumpet notes divide,

the Conscience of the People,
the symbol of our pride.
Anointing for the King, my child,
the sceptre,
orb, and crown;
with Princes bowing to the throne
in gartering and gown.
Insense a loyalty today
no folly can dissever.
God save the King,
our King, my child.
A king to live
for ever!

Death-dawn. Condemned. A City cockerel crows.
Take satisfaction, Adam, for your Fall!
Far from the garden now your folly grows:
Dear Simon's head in tears against the wall

And sleepless faces bawling in their rows
Yell blood. Is crucify their only call,
Indifference the sign that mercy shows?
Was this the measure of the cattle-stall,

The hills of Bethlehem in angelling
And shepherd's fear, denial disinterest here?
Adam, the crown, your King. Alone he stands,

Earth-battered. Adam's earthly Christ. A ring
Of Roman's burr—But see Barabbas stare
As pilate washes angels from his hands!

The Road

How helpless is God when Man is the master;
when God submits,
and Man asserts
his pride, a prelude to disaster.
How vainly Man gives God the blame
for all the violence
and the shame,
the failure of his fullest dreams,
the debris
of each broken cause,
the foetid earth
of futile wars.
Behind gay masks of mode and fashion,
doubt is fed,
the mob is mouthed;
Man's mastery become a passion :
those who are strong
will yell for death,
those who are strong will nurture needs :
if Good is God, then Good must bleed.

Master Man, how hard your head,
your heart so comfortless and cold.
How much infliction can I hold?
Your hardness still the instrument of pain—
O not your weakness :
weakness is not hard to bear;
I can comfort known despair.

Love, you are bared for us,
bleed for us.
Carry us, Gentle-Heart,
on to the hill :

our healing
your heaving,
the blood that you spill.
In the temper of time,
our failing
your falling :
Man's agression
the hammer and spear;
God's glory is empty,
is taught in the vice :
Man's mockery spins
in the soldier's dice.
Though we the torture,
the nail-driven pain,
give us a certainty, Love,
through our fears;
let an integrity calm us again.
Struggling, Simon in sorrow
is bowed.
Call out a Simon
in strength from the crowd.

You have turned my face westward
away from the city;
you have led me outside
the walls of your ease.
I have lived for you, Simon,
do what you please.
May there be love in you,
mercy,
and pity;
I have given you all
and you leave me to bleed;
the palms of my making
you nail to a bough,
a crown of your fashioning
thorns at my brow.
Take my submission. So
Simon
is freed.

The Cross

Three days till Easter.
The Money Market closed;
the typing pools in the City are silent.
Monday's hot favourite is exercised;
catamarans are out on the Solent.

Cars on the Special
Excursion are crammed.
How children laugh at the fish-leaping seals.
Ring roads through the suburbs are jammed;
Tridents take off for the Spanish Isles.

Hot Cross Buns.
Buy my Hot Cross Buns.
Four pennies.
Five pennies.
Hot
Cross
Buns.

On a trip down the Thames,
the cross on St. Paul's
is snapped as a "sight" from the Pleasure Cruises.
Knapsacks are packed for a hike through
the Dales;
the fisherman casts from the Pier and gazes.

Hot Cross Buns.
Buy my Hot Cross Buns.
Four pennies.
Five pennies.
Hot
Cross
Buns.

Now my hands hold you : Simon's work is done;
   Earth empties, dark on dark your death confirms.
   Here soldiers laughed; one cast, your raiment won.
Lie, my Son, tenderly, lie in my arms.

How once we fled the march of Herod's fear;
   those moments I recalled at times, you smiled :
   the shepherd's gaze, the Magi's gift of myrrh;
the nerve of Judas' kiss, now reconciled.

You would not have me weep? I weep. You wept
   for Lazarus. What city cost you tears?
   Rest in the garden now, so Simon slept.
Happy your humming executioners.

Lead on to love, where love to love is true.
   Lie still, my Child, may death meet life in you.

Father, forgive them.
  Father accept them
    Our Love will calm them.
Simon will lead them.
  Simon I claim as the measure of Man,
  measure of certainty,
    singleness,
      sanity;
Simon is Keeper,
      bestower,
        provider;
  Simon is Peter,
      the seal on the lock.
Simon will speak
      through the Doubter's despising.
  Simon, Love-strengthened,
        will tell of my rising.
Simon, the fisher, would never have chosen:
  Simon I chose.

Far from the casting net,
      anchor,
        and shore.

  Simon will own me
      through scaffold,
        through staves;
Simon will walk to me over the waves.

OCCASIONAL VERSES

Walsingham

Island of pity,
island of grace,
England has much in the mirror to face :
when Mary came to Walsingham,
this was a holy place.
When Mary came to Walsingham
she made an island blest,
made the Norfolk sky her own
that a heart might never hide alone,
a heart might find its rest.
For Mary came to show us home,
shelter of love and faith,
while in a trance
Richeldis knelt
and in her widowed longing felt
the calm of Nazareth.
By prayer and priest
the English east
became the beautiful,
the peaced.
the Little-House,
house of the poor,
where Mary liked to wait at the door
to see her children in.
Kings came,
ploughmen came,
pilgrims from Flanders and France;
turned with the tide
into Bishop's Lynn,
where river and quay,
as the ships veered in
rang with the Virgin's chants.
From wooded wold,

the fens,
and plain
the Chapel of St. Catherine
harboured the hungry and the lame;
and candel-led,
before his shame,
from Barsham Manor
Henry came
beside his rightful queen.
But men had eyes on Walsingham,
misers in want and wealth,
who for politics and power
would desecrate our Lady's Dower,
our sanity and health.
Those wreckers came to Walsingham,
one silent August day,
seeing the Little-House was sound,
they swiftly raised it to the ground
and Mary's image then they found
and rode with it away.
They burnt her image
for the crowd
in London,
where the hate was loud;
on Thames-side
Thomas Cromwell stood
and put to flames the precious wood
to pacify the proud.
"Weep, weep, O Walsingham
whose days are nights,
Blessing turned to blasphemies,
holy deeds to despites.
Sin is where Our Lady sat,
Heaven is turned to Hell,
Satan sits where Our Lord did stay
Walsingham, oh farewell."

Coda

Will we go to Walsingham,
    Will we give our time?
Will we draw on Mary's love
    In youth, old age, or prime?
And will we bring ourselves away
From Panorama or the play?
Must all we be, when weekends come,
    Blind pilgrims at the Stadium!

In Mary's land,
In England,
We'll shelter no denial,
But seek our home
In Walsingham,
Along the Holy Mile.

The Spider's Carol

for Monica

Hear the Spider on the wall
High above the cattle stall:
  "Mary, show your baby my
Carefully woven lullaby.

"Insects too have gifts to give
Though their ways are secretive;
  I, above His sleeping head,
Weave a Star of silken thread.

"Ox and Ass find honoured place,
Let the Spider share their grace,
  As Creation sees its Lord
By the Money Men ignored.

"This my small cobweb shall be
Something special made by me
  And I plead that Jesus might
Make it holy with His light.

"O that thought of Hope and Trust
Stirs a Spider made from dust,
  Fills my corner of the cave
With the smiles that Mary gave.

"Children, through your carolling
See my cobweb glistening;
  Join the Wise Men, and with them
Bring your Star to Bethlehem."

Maria

All that is gentle,
all that is strong
I need of you, my joy, Maria.
Gladden my grieving,
give me my song
safe from your hand,
Maria.
"This time is Our time",
I hear you say;
all the paths in your garden
lead one way,
your child in the centre
where you stand,
Maria.
Trust in my sorrow,
follow my flight
fast to your heart, my love, Maria.
Hasten your twelve stars
on my night,
your moon to my feet.
May England own you,
a garden again,
a rose in the hedgerow
after rain,
your child laughing with you
when we meet,
Maria.

The Lay of the Loser

1966

The sale cleared the debris of a winter day
and licked like cats
the possessor's boots;
the braces of the past held up for younger seats:
sowed-up like bags
the old inspired defeats.
And as the bald prices soared like stout sopranos,
we munched sandwiches
with cress flopped from our mouths
like whiskers on the charging Light Dragoons:
a printed battle bought and sold
and overcharged to Death.
Lot sixty-nine with cheese-dish, ladle, coffee spoons.
Fifteen pounds
for a worm-worked cradle,
where once a budding bishop sucked his bottle
towards a milk-white soul
who ended with the noose's sudden throttle.
O where moth and rust doth still corrupt. Who cares?
Sold to the gentleman
saying his prayers;
or is he bending, kneeling, feeling to undo his buckle?
O fat lady polishing the hallmark
with a stubby knuckle. Where thieves
break in and smash and grapple and grab. Who's
afraid of old Stocking-Face?
I am.
If I could have my wish, if I could choose,
I would like that butter-dish
and my heart's as heavy as a fireback.
Hark, hark, how the fire-dogs do bark, the dealers

are coming from town. In land-rovers, dormobiles,
car-back, bus-back. Fuel-mules.
That's for mustard, silly,
like my Aunty Guinivere. Take one meat-cover,
cut in half, screw in just above the shelf
and pop go the daffodils; and in summer,
pop go the geraniums. One sprig of silver holly
painted by the artist himself.
Going. Going. One packet of meat-frills.
One stag's head; but that was in another
country and besides the beast
is dead.
Another, shot by the artist's grandmother
wearing stays, before penicillin scotched the ague.
Come on, don't argue.
Lay nought up for yourself.
I thought it was silver. I could have sworn.
I bought it as silver
and now you say it's plate?
I said, don't argue. One four-poster,
one corroded electric toaster.
one Sheffield-plated coaster,
one copper chestnut roaster.
One Suffolk mezzotint,
one very mouldy print
and a black-framed, mounted poster: 1836,
assorted Georgian walking sticks.
As I said to George, why should
we worry? It's all insured.
All's well with the Midwives Immutable.
Phone for the midwives, Gordon.
One case of griffin-crested knives,
four newly-creosoted hives,
paper-backs in lots of fives.

The evening knarled the ear of the day
  and the tomcat's hackle-hair was up;
    the stars arched at twilight
  spitting into dusk. The wheat was golden
    now I gnaw the husk
  and wrap a blanket round my ankles like a house.
The sale has cleared the debris of defeat
  and felt the heart of unfamiliar rankles.
    O Death, you cower at every breath I'm on;
    Fond heart, drive on my weak pantechnicon.

The Wedding Guest

from The Albatross

It is the Angelus!
I stand. I sway! O free my silence from the sea,
you angling gulls! Drums, fuss
of brideful lights, clasped-hands and gamba-leaping knees,
dance on! A masque, a marriage through my prayer!
All grape-skull-gay, all flushed,
the guests as flagon-full as empty laughs. What tale?
What ribald song?—the muzzy Hall is hushed.—
Or does the Bridegroom kiss his Rose-Girl there?
But still the Storm-Blast comes! O see,
I cling to Marcy's sail!
so veil me, Virgin; save me, Mary!
Mariner!
Three strokes more! My stillness
eases, Lady. Tall as the spires, as the gong moon;
beyond, my words access.
This fix-amaze my offering! Ghost? Confusion
of corpse and spirit: let me understand
these horrors as a gift!
All honied for the feast, my heart upswelled and sang.
My speech as well prepared, I surely sniffed
contentment in the afternoon: the wedding band
unfiddled, tambourine, bassoon;
the Abbey belfry rang;
I paced in joy—till, England's June
unsleeved an autumn hand!

Again! Beside the stone
he pressed me on, the wrack my silence heaves across,
I kneel. "The word made Man",
my soul so cries. Commend me for my pain, my loss;
assure me that I balanced here before!
What desolation builds
me to this God; diminishings that rise above
the man my wishes planned? Do sorrowed fields
so scorn my cultured flowers? O by the Bird, restore
my Bridal calm! So less
I ask of succour, Love?
Sink down this summer albatross
that I take wing once more!

The Undertaker Poet

I am an Undertaker's Mate
And in this guise I serve the State;
For when I first began to sing
And grabbed Apollo by the wing
I learnt that Gods can trample hard
Across the longings of a Bard;
That none can propagate a fuss
Like those who drive the Delphic bus;
Until my love-lorn haggard lute
Began to sulk at lying mute.

Certain all remedy seemed lost,
The Orphic burrows crissed and crossed,
I searched the mountains, walls and beach,
Suffered my talent like a leech;
When in the hasting of the sea
The voice of Chance sang out to me:
"There is no cover for a Maker
As calm as Urban Undertaker."

Beside the coffin, flowers and hearse
I plan my salutary verse;
While solemn in my stove-pipe hat
I lap neat rhymes up like a cat;
Along the cluttered city roads
Settle my dithyrambs and odes
And at the traffic lights and jams
I stop and start in smooth iambs.
As often as the flames cremate

I kindle different ways to state
The reasons why my mind interns
Odd thoughts in carefully measured urns;

And as chaotic clangour yields
To country, cowslips, grass and fields,
Before they flutter off like birds
I trap Death's very truant words.
For those who willed an open grave
My panegyric mood I save;
While sometimes with the dust I throw
A friendly elegy or so;
For in Death's grim and giddy dance
It's nonsense to rely on chance.

Some chalk their fortune up to sense;
Others to long experience;
While some appear to trail bad luck.
The toys of Prospero and Puck,
Who justly blame their burden on
Fly Ariel or Oberon.
As if there weren't sufficient mirth
In tying girdles round the Earth
The Gods delight in watching Man
Cavort with lonely Caliban;
Or this is often how it seems:
The World the dark of Goddess' dreams.

For some time now this life I've led:
Poor, part-time Porter of the dead,
Of those released from fallen shame:
Cold, heavy nothings with a name.
There must be some who would not curse
The final triumph of a verse,

Who at the forfeiture of chance
Found words to match the limbless dance;
Reciting through a last despair
A poem as an act of prayer.

When you one day approach your grave,
A rebel still, at last Death's slave,
May you have in your very hearse
A poet thumping out his verse.